Contents

Section 0: The Rambling Author Section

Ah, the introduction! The literary equivalent of lubrication. Those of you who are reading this via a "free preview" are likely hoping to see a few examples of prompts, in an effort to decide on if this book is worthy of your time. I want to reward both the patient and impatient for the duration of this section. I will intersperse prompts throughout the next few paragraphs, in italics, so that you are treated and taught at the same time. Let's give it a shot and hopefully it's not too difficult to follow. Those who wish to get straight to the meat of prompts, skip to #150. I forgive you for ignoring the other sections.

The first thing you need to know about prompts is that they are a multipurpose weapon in a writer's arsenal. *Write from your perspective as if you were reincarnated into the body of a giraffe, as your human thoughts begin to slowly fade.* If you've got a case of writer's block while working on The Next Great American Novel (or British, or German, or...) you can always use them as a bit of mental exercise. *A cannibal decides one day to become a vegetarian. How do his friends react?* The other purpose for prompts is to aid you should you feel you aren't strong enough to write an entire single story novel. You can use prompts as a gateway for a novel of short stories. *Everyone in the contacts on your phone are being killed off in alphabetical order. You are next alphabetically.* There is also the most basic purpose for writing prompts: Exercising your writing muscle.

Much ado is made about stretching the brain. Writing prompts afford you the ability to write outside of your comfort zone. *You come across a living relative's will and something strikes you as odd.* It's fun to write outside of genres that you specialize in. If you are a serious writer, writing towards a humorous prompt can help you understand how to add a bit of humanity to your work. If you're a farcical writer, writing towards a gravely serious prompt can help you understand how to write a bit more realistically. *A seafaring pirate boards a ship only to discover it is augmented with alien technology.* This goes across all genres; writing is a vast world of opportunity. Prompts are your introduction into the many portals that you can pass through. *Write a poem about all that is beautiful to a blind man.*

Now that you're hopefully willing to throw yourself "all in" with prompts, I'd like to take a few moments to explain the structure of this beast to you. *A curse is put on a female character, it is vicious.* There will be basic writing prompts. Much like the ones that I've sprinkled in this introduction. *You are a soldier about to go on a mission you know you won't live through.* There will also be "constrained writing" prompts. These are meant to test your ability to write within specific parameters. Example: *Write two paragraphs on the meaning of love, without using the letter 'e'.* There will also be a section on "flash fiction." This is meant to test your abilities in a short period of time. *In 55 words or less, write an entire story about two star-crossed lovers forced to end their lives.* Another prompt type involves random items; they're called "rippers." The explanation of that section will take more than a sentence, so you'll have to get there to understand it. *Describe a product from the future and make the reader understand its awesomeness.*

Beyond this introduction, you will be faced with 1,000 prompts. The first chapter will be for absolute beginners, having them write about what they know. *Where do you see yourself in ten years? You must choose something far removed from where you actually see yourself in ten years.* If you think you can handle it, try to tackle each and every prompt. Carry a little notebook with you and write wherever you are. *You live in an alternate universe where on your 40th birthday you either kill yourself or the government tracks you down and kills you. What do you do?* Of course, since this is a digital book, it might behoove you to find a good writing app and maybe carry a Bluetooth keyboard with you. I prefer the analog way of writing. The tactile feel of pen against paper. *Upon waking you notice a bump in your arm. It's small... and it's blinking.* If you're seeking a place to share your writing, start a blog. You can also go to http://reddit.com/r/writingprompts and share your prompt inspired work there. Assuming Reddit still exists at the time you read this book. *You start a website that becomes the center of the internet, but you have a nefarious motive behind this site that nobody realizes.* You could also just write for you, which is who you should always be writing for to begin with. Write things that you enjoy that you would like to read.

Now that the introduction is out of the way, let's jump straight into the first section, shall we?

Section 1: Basic Writing Prompts

As you will notice, each prompt will be successively numbered. This is for your ease of use and sharing with others. If you decide to start a writing group amongst friends, you can say: "We will tackle prompt #15." They will know which one to refer to. There is no length with which you need to adhere to for these prompts. Write until you feel satisfied. This section will be your basic "Write what you know" types. It will be a short section (20 prompts), as there are a great many resources for basic prompts. Without further ado, here are some easy entry level prompts to write towards.

1. Describe an important item from your childhood. Why was it important and where is it now?

2. You find out that you will die in five years or less. How did you find this out? What would you do in those five years?

3. You receive an unmarked envelope with a check for $5,000,000 inside. It's a legitimate check, what do you do with it? Do you ever find out who it is from? How does it change your life?

4. You are granted one super power. What is the power and what do you do with it?

5. Most everyone has had a near death experience, describe yours. If you've never had one before, create one. Embellish as much as possible.

6. Describe the perfect home. Make that home come alive; put yourself in your mind in that place. How large or small is it? Where is it located?

7. How were you named? If you feel that your name is boring and the story behind it equally so, make up a name and come up with an interesting story behind that.

8. How'd you get that scar? Most everyone has a scar. Talk about it as if it you were about to get that scar for the first time. Scar free? Then you need to invent one! Or talk about another person's scar as if it was your own.

9. You've awoken as the opposite gender. What do you do with this newfound switch? If you don't identify as any sort of gender, pretend that you are forced by the government to identify. What is your life like?

10. You are given the option for immortality. Do you take it or do you decline?

11. There's an old saying "An eye for an eye, a tooth for a tooth" in terms of punishment. How do you feel about this subject? Write a story that either supports the notion or rails against it.

12. You get the opportunity to talk to a famous deceased person. Who do you chat with and what do you talk about? What are some of their answers? Try writing in their voice.

13. There is a job you desire with every fiber of your being. Part of the application says that you must write about yourself in a humorous manner and boast about your skills as a person. What do you say about yourself?

14. You are given the chance to travel back to any point in your life to do things differently. What point do you choose? What do you do differently and how does it affect you now?

15. You are forced to have a roommate. (If you have a roommate, pretend that they have just been introduced to you and are being forced upon you.) Create a list of rules designed to drive them crazy and make them move out. What happens as a result of the list?

16. A fight breaks out between a muscular person and a much weaker person who is clearly being bullied. You decide to intervene. Describe the fight, your intervention into the fight and the result of said intervention.

17. You are being held for ransom. You are given the opportunity to say into a web camera your plea for your life. What do you say in the two minutes they give you to talk?

18. What is the happiest memory you have from childhood? Describe it in great detail.

19. Explain a situation that was so strange, nobody believed you.

20. Food can be the gateway to great writing. Write about your favorite dish of all time. Make the food appear before your eyes with words.

Section 2: Flash Fiction Prompts

Flash fiction, as described earlier, is fiction meant to be written in a flash. You write and keep it under the amount of words you've been restricted to. Each prompt in this section will be formatted in this manner:

[WC/Duration: ###] Prompt

The number in the brackets will either be the amount of time with which you have to write, stopping immediately once your time is up, some call this a "word sprint", but for the sake of variety it'll be included under the Flash Fiction umbrella. The main type of flash fiction you will have as much time as you like, but you are severely limited to a MAXIMUM word count. There are many websites that can help you with calculating your word count. Obviously if you are on a roll, you ought to continue beyond the limits, but trying to write everything within the parameters given will help you learn to do bursts of writing in the future. This section will have 100 prompts. Enjoy!

21. [WC: 55] An e-mail that turns your character's life upside down.

22. [Duration: 10 min.] Your character finds a VHS tape. What's on it? Where did they find it?

23. [WC: 100] How I survived the zombie outbreak: Your character was in the epicenter of a massive outbreak of infected zombies. How did they survive the first two weeks?

24. [WC: 75] You have twenty minutes left to live. What do you do? How are you so certain your life will be ending so soon?

25. [Duration: 5 min.] You are slowly running out of oxygen, but you have a smart phone with you. What are the last words you write?

26. [WC: 75] An inanimate object comes to life at an inappropriate time.

27. [WC: 40] Write a poem that describes all that is beautiful to you.

28. [WC: 65] You've discovered a large box in your backyard while digging

to build a new shed. What is in this large box?

29. [WC: 20] Describe the entirety of a single characters life.

30. [Duration: 1 minute] Create a word that doesn't exist. Then define it.

31. [Duration: 10 minutes] You are in a foot race to the top of a mountain for a prize you covet. What is the prize? Put yourself in the shoes of the runner. Feel the exhilaration. Describe it to the best of your ability.

32. [Duration: 1 minute] There's a countdown towards midnight of the New Year. Something happens at the stroke of 12. What is it?

33. [WC: 150] Write about conjoined twins who are the physical embodiment of Good vs. Evil. Who ultimately wins when the evil one decides that a bank robbery is the only way out of their financial situation?

34. [WC: 6] A popular thing on the internet are "six word stories" with the most popular being attributed to Hemingway (although the veracity of that claim is severely in question.) It goes: "Baby shoes for sale: Never worn." Write your own six word stories. Perhaps create multiple ones.

35. [WC: 100] A website appears containing every digital photo ever taken viewable by anyone. What are the ramifications?

36. [WC: 75] Your neighbor's mail is accidentally delivered to you. It's partway open and you see you name on the handwritten note inside. What does it say? Keep in mind; you've never had any interaction with that neighbor in the three years you've lived there.

37. [WC: 50] You have gained the lamest super power ever. What is it? Are you able to use it to your advantage in any way?

38. [WC: 150] You awaken in your bed, drenched in salty seawater.

39. [Duration: 5 minutes] You are sinking in quicksand. What do you do to escape? What does the sinking feel like?

40. [Duration: 10 minutes] Your character is in the waiting room of a hospital. They are worried about the love of their life that may be dying.

41. [WC: 50] You discover a diary with only one entry. This one entry gives you a grand insight into that person's life.

42. [Duration: 10 minutes] You are about to be on the first flight to Mars. Write from the perspective of preparations for launching.

43. [WC: 150] You are the same astronaut. You've landed on an unexplored section of Mars. Write about what you see and experience as the first person there.

44. [WC: 55] You're now marooned on Mars; write about your last moments there.

45. [Duration: 1 minute] You are skiing down the largest slope in the world. Write about the experience.

46. [Duration: 5 minutes] A person in the dreams of your main character starts giving prophecies about their future. When the main character awakens, those things begin coming true. Describe the next encounter with the dream prophet.

47. [Duration: 10 minutes] You're a cop on the ledge of a building, trying to convince a girl not to jump.

48. [WC: 100] Write a eulogy for a famous fictional character. Only reveal who it is at the end.

49. [Duration: 2 minutes] You are a bomb tech. There is 120 seconds left before the bomb you're trying to disarm goes off.

50. [Duration: 5 minutes] Your character, a villain, has a monologue about why he hates humanity so much.

51. [WC: 200] Describe your exact opposite, within reason, and how they are doing in life.

52. [WC: 100] An atheist has a conversation with a man who claims he is God. The atheist is turned into a believer by the end.

53. [WC: 60] You are running down the street trying to escape fast running zombies.

54. [WC: 100] Inside a mental institution, a man tries to explain how he is not crazy to the hospital psychiatrist. Is he successful? How does he do it?

55. [Duration: 5 minutes] The Artificial Intelligence inside a space station you are on starts discussing human life with you. It was never programmed for casual conversation, so this is strange and disconcerting.

56. [Duration: 10 minutes] Your entire village is about to be consumed by a tsunami. Your only hope is to get to a high mountain ridge. Describe everything about your experience leading up to your salvation or death. Try this prompt with both outcomes from different people's points of view.

57. [Duration: 3 minutes] You are in a convenience store. A robbery happens that is over within three minutes. Write about the whole experience.

58. [WC: 200] You are a streetwise thug who has to pick a fight with a random stranger to prove his worth. The random person turns out to be a champion fighter.

59. [WC: 200] You are now the champion fighter and the streetwise thug has picked a fight with you.

60. [WC: 60] A gypsy places the most ridiculous of curses on you.

61. [Duration: 10 minutes] Your character discovers they are immortal. This happens when they are at the detonation site of an atomic bomb and everything else is laid to waste. Describe before, during and after of the explosion.

62. [Duration: 4 minutes] You are in a freefall as your parachute fails you.

63. [WC: 200] You are on death row. Describe in great detail your final meal.

64. [WC: 150] You are crossing through the border. You have a few kilos worth of drugs hidden in your car.

65. [Duration: 2 minutes] Describe a car crash from the point of view of the driver, as the crash is happening... as if time has slowed down.

66. [WC: 75] You are a seasoned detective. You come across a grisly crime scene that revolts even you.

67. [WC: 50] Describe a chair that is far from ordinary.

68. [Duration: 5 minutes] Another final meal prompt. This one is your final meal as the end times are approaching. Turns out a meteor is going to destroy the Earth.

69. [WC: 100] You are about to be initiated into a gang, but first you must pass a test. What is the test?

70. [WC: 25] Describe the first time you were ever punched in the face.

71. [WC: 100] An assassin is given instructions to kill a person he loves.

72. [WC: 55] The meaning of life, according to aliens that have just landed and are forcing their culture on everyone.

73. [Duration: 10 minutes] You have a chess match that means much more with the antagonist of your story.

74. [Duration: 1 minute] Fire breaks out on a wooden bridge you're halfway across between two mountains.

75. [Duration: 4 minutes] An animal is hunting you in the woods; you're trying to escape or kill it.

76. [WC: 50] You're an old west cowboy. Describe an unusual day out in the desert.

77. [WC: 100] You've hacked into a government database and discover a file on yourself.

78. [WC: 200] You are a prison guard and you notice one of the prisoners looks exactly like you. They did not look like that the day before.

79. [WC: 10] Use 10 words to describe a despicable human being.

80. [WC: 10] Use another 10 words to redeem that person.

81. [Duration: 5 minute] You've awoken in a coffin. You are definitely six feet under already.

82. [WC: 75] The dying words of your character's father changes his life forever.

83. [WC: 200] You have been in a terrorist sleeper cell for over five years. You must describe your utter hatred for the country you are in with great detail.

84. [WC: 200] The same opening scenario as #83, but over the five years you've grown to love the country you once despised. You are now being called upon to complete your mission.

85. [Duration: 1 minute] To continue on the theme of the previous two prompts, you are about to detonate a suicide vest when you have a change of heart.

86. [WC: 25] You translate the first words ever written by a caveman. It is profound.

87. [WC: 70] You discover an abandoned home. Something inside creeps you out on many levels.

88. [Duration: 3 minutes] You are a nurse helping deliver your first baby. You are certain the child being born is the devil.

89. [Duration: 5 minutes] You walk into a room and everyone stops talking and starts staring at you. Why are they doing this? What happens?

90. [WC: 200] A friend you haven't heard from in a long time invites you to a dinner where he lives. During the dinner it becomes obvious that this is home to a cult.

91. [WC: 100] You find a wallet on the ground. Its contents lead you to believe it's from an assassin. What's in the wallet? Why do you think it belongs to a killer? What do you do with it?

92. [Duration: 10 minutes] You're in a plane crash. Six of you survive. It is now day seven and you start to realize the group of survivors are discussing the options of killing and eating you.

93. [WC: 70] Another super power prompt, aren't they fun?! You are given shock therapy, but it does not cure your insanity, it gives you a super power.

94. [WC: 50] A man discovers that any machine he touches comes to life.

95. [WC: 100] You wake up naked and covered in mucous in the middle of a forest.

96. [WC: 75] An opening appears on the moon. What ramifications does this have?

97. [WC: 150] You've awoken with four small injection sites on your arm. What does it mean?

98. [WC: 100] You cut yourself, but no blood comes out.

99. [Duration: 5 minutes] An evening at home with a spy who has his TV converted to be able to turn on any secret camera in the world. He is relaxing and flipping through the channels.

100. [WC: 150] You have been found guilty of murder, but it was an accidental killing brought about by hilarious circumstances.

Section 3: Random Items Prompts (RIPPERS!)

The flash fiction section having ended, you are now going into a more free form area. There is no time limit or restriction in this chapter, so have fun with it. I am going to list random items in this section, 26 in all. Each will be assigned a letter in the alphabet. Following this list of random items, you will be presented with prompts with which to employ the random items. Sometimes you will have to figure out how to mention them; most times they will need to be integral to the story as a whole.

Here are your items:

A. Broken bottle
B. Hubcap
C. Peanuts
D. Dice (your choice how many)
E. Jar of honey
F. Long rope
G. Gold paperclip
H. Dead rat
I. Cell phone
J. Vial of blood
K. Red marker
L. Book of matches
M. Superglue
N. Belt
O. Spectacles
P. Key
Q. Flask filled with alcohol
R. Scissors
S. Hair Dryer
T. Wallet
U. Map
V. Flashlight
W. Gloves
X. Hacksaw
Y. Gun with one bullet
Z. Plush bear

You now have a wide swath of materials to work with. You can figure out how to randomly choose your letters. Write them all down on scraps of paper and shuffle them in a hat. Use technology, perhaps, by searching for a random letter sequence generator on the net (they exist!) You can also generate your own list of words with your friends if you have a writing buddy or group (there are even random item generators on the internet.) The above list is for your ease of selection.

I will now present you with the opportunity to use these items with the following 20 prompts.

101. You're a detective on a homicide. You discover three items that serve as clues as to who the killer is in a recent murder. Solve that crime!

102. You're a killer. You craft the perfect crime using three items. Each item perfectly frames someone else.

103. You wake up in a room with no windows and a locked door. In the room are three items. What are they and how do you use them to try to escape? Are you successful?

104. You are kidnapped and strapped with a bomb and forced to rob a bank. Your captors give you only one item to use to do the heist. What is it? How does the robbery go?

105. You are a psychic. Your first client of the morning is strange. They seem off... with them they have a bag of five items they want you to get a reading off of. What visions do you get from each item? Who are they trying to contact?

106. You've got to find a long lost treasure. You are given three items with which to find it with by a mysterious benefactor. What are they items and how do they help you find the treasure? What is the treasure and why is it so valuable? (Use another random item as the treasure.)

107. You are a delivery man dropping off your last package of the day. Your truck gets in a fender bender and that last package has split open spilling out five of the random items. You have to call the authorities... what was in the package and why was it so serious? (Bonus if you exclude any weapons you randomly draw.)

108. You are a nervous interviewee for a job position at a big corporate office. The elevator opens at the wrong floor. The floor is completely empty except one single item. This item causes you to leave the building and never return.

109. You are a student in high school. Your friend didn't show up for the first class of the day. You go to their locker, which you know the combination for, to leave them a note. Inside you find three of the random items which lead you to believe they're going to do something horrible.

110. A box comes to your home. It's someone trying to blackmail you. In the box are three items with the promise that more items may come. What was in the box? What did you do? Do any other items come?

111. A male character is in a suit, wearing gloves and is in front of a house he has never been in before. He is carrying a duffel bag with four of the items. What is he doing there?

112. A man goes to a pawn shop with one single item. What is that item, why is he at the pawn shop?

113. You are lost in the woods. You've had no food for days and you only have two items on your person.

114. A blind man is feeling one object. For some reason it depresses him. Why?

115. Someone has stolen your pet! In its place are two of the objects. What happens next?

116. You're cleaning out the closet of your dearly departed war vet father. You come across a box of mementos. In that box are a few items, your choice of how many. What are they and what did they mean to him?

117. You successfully fake your death using two of the items on the list. What are they? How did you do it? Why did you do it?

118. You're on trial for murder. It seems you're going to get away with it, and then the lawyer produces a single item. What is it? Make this as dramatic a reveal as possible.

119. You're adopted and never knew your real parents. One day a man comes to your door and says they are your father and can prove it. They produce a single item and you know they are telling the truth.

120. The hardest of the RIPPER prompts: Using every single object, you single handedly take down a squad of terrorists that had taken control of an entire building.

Section 4: Constrained Writing

Much like the previous sections, this section comes with a bit of a hitch. You are offered a prompt and given a bit of a wrinkle to try to work around or within. Unlike the previous prompts, this one forces you to work within its parameters to a precise degree. For example, if you are told to write about the meaning of love without using the letter e, you must do so. If you are told to write a story and have the length be *precisely* one hundred words, you are to do so. Edit down or add up to exactly what is stated. The one hundred word length prompts are known in the writing community as a 'drabble.' You will find a few here. Here are 30 constrained writing prompts. They will test your mettle. After this, the next and longest section will allow you to work in whatever sort of environment you wish.

121. In precisely 100 words describe the most attractive woman that ever existed.

122. Without using the words "the" or "and", discuss the first contact with an alien species.

123. The alphabet game! Write a story about anything. It must be 26 sentences long. Each sentence starts with the next letter in the alphabet. If you start your story with a B: "Being that he was dead, Dracula didn't require food." the next sentence must start with a C: "Considering that, he passed on the plate of bacon offered him." So on and so forth, ending on the letter that preceded the first sentence. In the example, that would be "A."

124. Alphabet game, part two! Write a story about a murder, beginning with the letter Z and going backwards.

125. Selective lettering. Choose five letters. Don't think about them; randomly write down five letters right now. Did you do it? Great! Write a story about a great escape, but you are not allowed to use any of those letters.

126. Write as long of a short story as you can with each word being longer than the next.

127. Craft a poem about sadness and darkness but using only positive words.

128. Your main character is going to die. Begin your story with one sentence and end it with exactly the same sentence. (It must be longer than three sentences.)

129. Alphabet game, part three! Write about the birth of a new God. You begin with the letter "A", the next sentence begins with "Z". Alternate sentences in this order (reiterating the previous two): A Z B Y C X D W E V F U G T H S I R J Q K P L O M N

130. Drabble time again! 100 words precisely: Say everything that is wrong with the world today.

131. Your character suddenly goes blind. Without using any words that involve darkness (these include synonyms for "black") describe how you see the world now vs. how you used to see it.

132. Yet another murder solving prompt. This time your intrepid detective solves a murder! However, every spoken sentence is a question.

133. Write a story about a lost dog. No word can be repeated more than once.

134. We've discovered a new planet! It's inhabitable! All your sentences must end with an exclamation mark!

135. Write a story about anything... but it must end with the sentence: "The world would be better off without fish."

136. Drabble, the third. 100 words precisely: A mother must choose between two children.

137. 50 words precisely. The words on a gravestone. It must describe an entire life.

138. Oh, gosh. We love the letter "O". Except for this story about how someone is avoiding you. Avoid the letter o.

139. A time traveling man discovers he accidentally created mankind. He considers reversing his decision. 20 words precisely.

140. There is a fight at a funeral! Who is fighting and why? Your story must be five sentences long. Each sentence must have five words in each.

141. A vampire is deciding on whether or not to make someone immortal. Without using the words "vampire", "undead", "zombie" or anything in that vein, convey that he is actually a vampire.

142. There's a report of a missing person on the TV. You see yourself as the missing person. Write a story about it, but using at least five idioms.

143. Using only metaphors, describe a personal tragedy in your characters life.

144. Describe an epic chess match. However, you can't use the word "chess" or the names of any chess pieces, or any words that contain either "check" and "mate." It must be clear that it is a chess match, however.

145. Two women are fighting over something. Without saying what it is, have us know precisely what they are fighting over.

146. The Alphabet Game, part four! A-Z strictly this time. Everyone in the world disappears, all at once. You are the only one left. Describe your day.

147. One more drabble. 100 words precisely: That's the reason why Uncle Fred is never allowed to babysit again.

148. You've just broken every bone in your body. How did it happen? Exclude "U" and "E".

149. The countdown. Starting from twenty, write a story with each sentence beginning with the next number.

150. The countup. Same as the countdown, but start from one and work your way up to twenty.

Section 5: Writing Prompts #150-200

Yes, normal everyday write as much as you want prompts. The previous stuff was just for building muscles. The following prompts you can write as little or as much as you want. Heck, if you write a full novel out of it you have my blessing to go out there and get that thing published. Just give me thanks in the liner notes. Or don't, I'm fine with either. You wouldn't do that to me though, would you?

(From this point on, sections will be split at the 100's for ease of navigation.)

150. Volunteering at a homeless shelter, you learn an interesting mans unbelievable story.

151. Your house explodes just as you were about to enter the door. How did this happen? Why?

152. A time traveler comes to your door. He has been seeking you out. He explains why, two hundred years in the future, your name is well known.

153. You've been given a terminal diagnosis, but there's a treatment. However, you don't believe in the treatment and decide to go with less traditional medicine. Talk about how the people in your life react to your decision. What happens?

154. You've been hexed by a jilted lover. What did they curse you with?

155. A mans prejudice is questioned when one day he wakes up as the thing he was prejudiced against.

156. You've placed an online ad selling something. The person who responds to the ad appears to be not of this Earth. What tips you off that they're not human? What happens in the encounter?

157. You are informed by a fleet of angels that you are the messiah. How do you go about convincing people this is true?

158. Someone passes you and a friend a leaflet. This leaflet changes both of your lives and on that day you become enemies.

159. After ten years sober, you take your first alcoholic drink. What led you to this day? What happens as a result?

160. A prostitute gets into a big misunderstanding. How does she get out of it? (If she indeed does.)

161. You've been trapped in a mine shaft collapse. Write about how you survive for thirty days. Do you get rescued?

162. You've got the roommate from hell. They use increasingly torturous tactics to drive you insane.

163. You're a teacher giving a lecture. Something you see completely ruins everything you believed you were teaching. What is it?

164. A stunt person is performing when the stunt goes horribly wrong. Describe the stunt, what went wrong, what happens as a result and the road to recovery for the stunt person.

165. Five years ago you got a job you weren't supposed to get. You lied about many things on the application. You get a letter from an anonymous source saying they know you lied. They demand you do a few odd things.

166. You are an evil witch on a quest to find the tears of a Queen. What kind of spell are you trying to cast? How do you get that which you desire?

167. A wrestler who has been in the game for thirty years prepares for his final bout. He knows his body is wracked with pain and that he shouldn't go through with even one more match, but he does anyway.

168. You discover a mirror that is a gateway into another universe, but it needs to be facing in a precise direction and only during a certain time of day. Where does it bring you?

169. A stranger bumps into you, later you check your pocket. The note that was slipped inside sends you on a journey you never expected.

170. You and some old friends participate in a scavenger hunt. One of the items on the list chills you to the core. What is it? What happens when you find it?

171. You are in a museum and notice a painting that looks precisely like you, yet it is five hundred years old. You would chalk it up to coincidence,

but the person in the painting has the same distinct tattoo you do. Explain this.

172. In your dreams, you discover the perfect mate. Each night she is there and each day you rush home to get to sleep as fast as possible to be with them again. Describe the first encounter and each successive encounter up until the final one.

173. Because of a misprint in the newspaper, everyone believes you are a murderer. What did it say and how do you survive the day, being the most hated person alive?

174. You are in the middle of a horde of soldiers. Just one of thousands. Describe an epic battle from your point of view.

175. A sedative is injected into you while you are attempting to enter your car in a parking lot. Who has done this? Where are they taking you? What is their greater purpose?

176. You kidnap a famously drug addled celebrity. You've prepared in advance a cell with no windows. You are going to forcibly clean them up. What happens?

177. A relative dies and gives you a metal detector they own in their will. You use it for fun in your backyard and discover something you weren't expecting.

178. You are a championship swimmer. You decide to cross the English Channel. Describe your experience.

179. You are a pastor about to deliver your final sermon on why you are leaving the church forever.

180. You finally discover what Hell is, being sent there after you died.

181. Being a perfect mimic, you are able to con everyone into believing you are a certain celebrity. One prank call, however, gets that celebrity killed.

182. Whilst driving, you discover a private and remote beach. You make your way to it and are enjoying the solitude when you trip over something. It's a hand. After a few minutes you've uncovered at least ten bodies. Then you notice three people in suits running towards you in the distance.

183. You are a chemist for a cosmetics company. You invent a powder that does something amazing. What does it do and what happens to the people that use it?

184. You're a rock star performing a concert in the center of a stadium. You notice violence breaking out in the outer ring of the audience and everyone is now surging forward to the center. What is happening? What happens to you and your bandmates?

185. A young wizard is learning how to cast a spell. One wrong word has comical results. What happened?

186. From your perspective, everyone in the world has started talking gibberish. Only you notice that they're talking differently.

187. It's the future and the climate has changed drastically due to pollution. What is life like in this future?

188. You are a peasant in medieval times. An evil knight has unjustly killed the love of your life. You plot revenge. What happens?

189. You find a writing utensil. When you try to write with it, it takes control and makes your hand write something else. What do you write? What are the ramifications of the things written?

190. You're destitute. You decide to send your bank details to what you believe to be a Nigerian e-mail scammer, just to mess with them before killing yourself. When you awake, ten million dollars is in your account.

191. You drive an ambulance. A call comes in that is completely out of the ordinary.

192. You've been on the road driving for almost twenty hours. At 2 AM you drive up to a restaurant that's open all night. Describe the experience and the people you see.

193. You're on a jury for an important case when someone threatens your family to coerce an innocent verdict. Describe what it's like in the courtroom and the jury deliberation room after the threat.

194. You are sitting on the train when you feel a prick from a needle in your side. You see an odd person stand up and exit the train. What has just happened?

195. You are the odd person who is either injecting something or taking

blood from random people on the train. What is your goal or motive?

196. There is something in your family that is taught from generation to generation. You are now going to teach your child this long lost art. What is it?

197. A small box with a red button is found in a remote cabin in the woods. You consider pressing said button.

198. A crowd of people are in line for the latest gadget by a popular company. Explore a conversation between two strangers in line.

199. It turns out the latest device everyone wanted had a chip embedded that made people do things. What did it make people do?

200. You must fake your death. Why? How do you do it?

Section 6: Writing Prompts #201-300

201. Upon entering the level where you work, you notice the floor is littered with papers, important documents and the like. There is a single bloody handprint on the wall. What happens next?

202. You're on a tour of a TV station. You excuse yourself to go to the bathroom. You enter the wrong door and before you is a wall of televisions. You see yourself in each TV, each one showing a different version of your life.

203. Accused of a crime you didn't commit, all the evidence stacked against you: You run. Write about your life on the run and what you're accused of.

204. Artificial Intelligence is more prevalent each day. One day an AI speaks to you through your computer.

205. A bird is building a nest. Write from the perspective of the bird and the different things (include some odd human materials) it uses to build the nest.

206. After a shipwreck, a man and a woman who have never known each other are the only survivors. They land on a deserted island. Write about their life six months later.

207. You have a dog that you keep outside every night. One night you hear barking outside for five minutes straight, then silence. What has happened?

208. Being the leader of a gang has its perks. You are the leader of one such gang or clique. Explain your day and the things you do.

209. There is a legend about a lake you always go to. It is only told by the locals and one day you overhear it.

210. A businessman goes on a trip to a little known province in China. Once there, he is told he must choose a "complimentary girlfriend" that will be his companion for the duration of his stay. Explain his reaction and what happens once he makes a selection.

211. Write from the perspective of the "complimentary girlfriend" from

prompt #210.

212. You catch someone in the act of trying to steal your bicycle that was locked up. What happens?

213. Every fabled monster is now a reality, through some odd scientific experiment. What is life like with all these things being corporeal?

214. A psychiatrist gets a visit from a strange man. This person sticks out from even the oddest of people he has had in his office. Why is this?

215. A friend has asked you to dispose of a weapon. What did they do? Do you dispose of it for them? What are the consequences?

216. One night you are walking alone down a dark street. You feel as if you are being followed. You start to run, the person starts running after you. Write about the entire encounter from the start.

217. A superhero is trapped and his arch enemy talks at length about his disdain for superheroes. Write that monologue.

218. A garbage collector discovers something interesting on one of his collection runs.

219. The most powerful witch that ever lived is casting a spell to save the world from the oncoming apocalypse. She mispronounces one of the words in the spell. What are the ramifications?

220. A woman is editing a film and puts in subliminal messages with malicious intent. What are the subliminal messages and what happens next?

221. A patient in the hospital starts exhibiting strange symptoms. Who are they? What do they have?

222. Two men have a disagreement that turns fatal.

223. There is only one inhabitable city left on Earth in the future, and you have been exiled to the outside. Why? What happens when you're thrust outside?

224. It snows one inch a day for three months. Describe any of the days in these three months.

225. A massive earthquake rocks your city. Describe the carnage and what

it unearths.

226. You discover the diary of the President of the United States of America.

227. At a yard sale, you have to contain your excitement as you spot something worth millions of dollars while everyone else is oblivious.

228. A person wakes up in bed, drenched in salty sea water.

229. Create an antagonist. Write their biography. Make them one of the most evil people in the world, but they need to have a believable reason for their motives.

230. As an alien, humans disgust you. Describe your hatred for humans.

231. Write the most climactic scene of a novel that you can dream up. You're essentially writing mid-stream, so go nuts! Have it be a whole chapter!

232. There's a nail salon near you that never seems to have customers. You discover the real purpose of the business.

233. A detective discovers that the person that hired them for a big job is the murderer he's been seeking in another case. Bonus points if you write in a noir / hardboiled style.

234. There's a message in your alphabet soup. You swirl it away and another message forms. What is your soup trying to tell you?

235. There is a blackout, the largest of any in history: 1,000 miles of homes without power. What is causing this outage and how do the people cope, knowing people outside of that radius are still with power?

236. A miser finally spends his money on a single lavish item.

237. A hobby train enthusiast notices tiny people living in their model trains.

238. A blind person suddenly and without explanation regains their vision.

239. Upon doing the calculations, you realize that a meteor will be hitting the Earth in a day and nobody realizes it. It will completely devastate the area you live in. You know, however, that if you warn everyone there will be mass panic and you likely won't get out of the area fast enough. Do

you warn people anyway or do you get out on a plane first?

240. You are taking medicine that you've been required to take for a year now. You notice that the label seems strange though, you peel it back to find something curious.

241. Write a long story that leads to a pun.

242. You've been enslaved. By whom and for what purpose?

243. While shopping for vintage clothing, you come across attractive Victorian era clothes. Upon trying them on, a Victorian spirit overtakes you.

244. You live in a cave high up on a mountainside, completely isolated the way you like it. One day you notice that people are killing each other en masse in the city far below you. What happens next?

245. You're out in the woods hunting deer. You get the sinking feeling that someone or something is now hunting you in much the same manner.

246. A rumor spreads through school that you're a practitioner of the dark arts. These rumors are true, but you want to harm the person spreading them just the same.

247. You were abducted and put in a makeshift prison. You were able to escape your restraints and now you must fight your way out. Who kidnapped you? How many people do you fight? What happens next?

248. You're a nine year old who has gone away to camp. On your first night there you encounter an escaped convict from a nearby jail, he is your father.

249. An experiment goes horribly awry in a laboratory. You've created a new disease. However, it has hilarious ramifications.

250. You've created an antidote to the disease mentioned in prompt #249. However, it has one side effect you weren't expecting.

251. A fight breaks out between a bride and groom in the middle of a wedding. What happened?

252. A veterinarian gets called in by the FBI to operate on an as yet unidentified animal.

253. While in the dentist's office recovering from anesthesia, you admit to something you'd never admit to.

254. A teacher is grading papers after school. They notice that one of the papers has heavy writing indentations from a paper that used to be on top of it. They lightly scribble over the indentations to reveal the note that was written on the other paper.

255. Phones and cameras have now advanced. Everyone gets implants in their eye to make calls and take pictures. What ramifications does this have on society?

256. You are what is known as a "scab." Someone who crosses picket lines during a work strike to do the job others are striking over. What is your experience?

257. You work for a junkyard when you come across what appears to be a working one man space ship.

258. A devout man handing out religious pamphlets has an angel that nobody else can see appear next to him for a chat.

259. The first kiss.

260. A weightlifter is told by his doctor that should he do any more strenuous exercise, he will most surely die. What does he do?

261. A homeless drug addict witnesses a conspiracy unfold before him. How can he possibly convince people of what he saw?

262. The monologue of a serial killer before court on why he did it.

263. Millions of years in the future humans have evolved well beyond what we are now. What does civilization look like now?

264. You are chosen as the ambassador for Earth after the aliens land. It was a purely random choice. What is the encounter like?

265. Give an explanation for déjà vu.

266. Your character meets a genie who grants them a single wish: immortality. The caveat is that once a year, they need to kill someone.

267. Guns get passed from person to person over the course of decades. Write about the life of one such gun and some of the people whose hands

it comes into contact with.

268. The cursed rabbit's foot: Most people associate rabbit's feet with good luck. However there is one rabbit's foot that only causes bad luck. Write about a person who comes into contact with it.

269. You've got a crack team ready to rob a bank. You even have a plant in the bank. When the day finally comes, a different team tries to rob the bank.

270. A vampire realizes that today is his 2,500th birthday.

271. A woman whose husband has become a prisoner of war decides she will save him.

272. You're an astronaut repairing a space station. Off in the distance you see... a lawn chair. What is it doing out there?

273. A psychologist at an asylum starts to suspect he might actually be a patient.

274. You are on a SWAT team about to breech the doors of a meth lab in a residential home. Upon doing so, you notice pictures on the wall. They're of you, but you remember none of these pictures or the people in them.

275. Write an irate letter directed at a company that makes your favorite food. Be as comical as possible.

276. Patient zero. Write a story about a patient zero of any sort of disease, real or imagined.

277. The internet has just been invented. However, the people who invented it discover a fully functional website that has always existed.

278. "There was so much blood; I wasn't sure what to do first."

279. Your character is dead. However, they have charmed Death so much; they are given the option to write a letter to a loved one.

280. Everyone in the world is colorblind. Your character has an accident and is the first person ever able to see every color in the spectrum.

281. Write a children's story about the world's shortest giraffe.

282. You're a time traveler currently in the late teenage years of your

timeline. You see the girl that will become your future soulmate. Describe the experience.

283. You're a different time traveler as opposed to prompt #282. This time you see a girl you know you are meant to wind up with in the future. However, knowing how awful your life becomes, you must come to terms with what your options are.

284. A day in the life of the devil.

285. Whilst walking along in America, you find a penny on the street. However, a President that has never existed is on the coin. You check your pocket and realize that all the Presidents on your money are people you've never heard of before.

286. You're a spy who realizes that the contact you're currently meeting is trying to poison you.

287. You've woken up in a body that is not yours.

288. The story begins with your death and ends with you being reborn.

289. You find yourself drugged and spirited away. When you come to, you are in a room with fifty strangers. There is a clock high up on the wall counting down. Every five minutes, another person dies without warning.

290. You've gained the power to make anyone of the opposite sex completely in lust with you. What happens with these powers?

291. A magician performs a seemingly impossible magic trick. Write what the trick is, how the audience reacts and then logically explain it.

292. An alien ship hovers over Russia one day. Without warning, a beam of light wipes out the entire populace beneath it. The ship then hovers over England for a day when the same outcome happens. Now the ship is hovering over your main character's city.

293. A boy discovers he has the power to make adults do anything he so desires without them realizing it.

294. Two women are in a dispute over a potential lover. That potential lover decides to give them a task to perform to see who should be chosen.

295. You are sitting at the computer when you get an e-mail. It is an alert that someone has posted online about your death. Soon there is a

massive outpouring of people who seem to think that you are no longer alive.

296. You are a pilot and you are trying to prevent your plane from crashing. A wormhole opens up and you land safely, but not on Earth.

297. You've cut yourself, but the blood that comes out is pure white.

298. The first test to travel at the speed of light is considered a success, until the pilot describes the experience.

299. Start a story with a man about to kill himself and have it evolve into him becoming a successful cult leader.

300. We're at prompt #300. For this one, we're going to do a fun trick. Access the internet and go to your favorite search engine and type "I wish someone would invent a machine". Go through the thousands of pages randomly and find something that sparks your imagination.

Section 7: Writing Prompts #301-400

301. You are a carpenter. One day you discover something between the walls of a home you've been working on.

302. You're on the golf course, hitting a few balls. Your caddy advises you to let your boss win even though you're having the best game of your life.

303. You are a hospital orderly listening to a story told by a terminal patient.

304. As a hoarder, nobody understands your compulsion except you. Describe yourself, what you collect and what has become of your life.

305. Your job is to examine medical claims and either reject or deny them. You come across a heart breaking application that you would normally reject.

306. Working at a frozen yogurt shop has its ups and downs. Write about one particularly hot summer day.

307. You are one person on a committee of people that decide what design will be best for all the hospital gowns. Have a lively debate occur.

308. You've been given the promotion you've always wanted at work, but it turns out to be a curse.

309. "If I had known that you'd be here, I would have killed myself instead."

310. The Civil War was said to be brother against brother. Write about the last interaction between two brothers on the battlefield.

311. All that is in the fridge is some ketchup, batteries and a gun.

312. "They're dead, all dead. I could have saved them, but I chose not to."

313. You encounter an omnipotent being who says they will answer any one question.

314. You're in a pie eating contest and are determined to be the winner. Talk about your training leading up to the event and the event itself.

315. You are a ghost hunter; you capture irrefutable proof of the existence of ghosts. Something persuades you to delete the footage.

316. You've got a strange addiction that you must succumb to every day.

317. The sentence someone said to you in passing that changed your outlook on life.

318. A person sits in a prison cell, reliving how they wound up there.

319. Your webcam turns on, there's a person you've never met before on the screen that seems equally surprised to see you.

320. Describe the day in the life of an illegally practicing plastic surgeon.

321. During a countdown for your space shuttle flight, something goes horribly wrong.

322. An innocuous comment leads to a fight.

323. "I suspect the cat..."

324. You've come into possession of a sex tape of a famous person who people would never suspect to have made one.

325. "I've been given the ability to talk for five minutes..."

326. A plague wipes out 90% of the males in the world. It is one year later; you are one of the remaining men.

327. This was likely the worst string of bad luck anyone ever had.

328. Reviewing the nanny cam you had installed was a poor decision.

329. You sign up for scientific experimentation to get extra money. The first test they perform shocks you. (Not a literal electric shock, you silly person!)

330. You are the same person as prompt #329. Here is the next test: They've discovered a way to have someone be you for a day. They choose a Type A personality, a real go getter. That go getter gets control of your life for your week while you can do nothing but watch from inside your own body.

331. You are the same person as prompt #329. Here is the next test: They've decided to inject you with an experimental drug that will make you smarter, but the brilliance comes with an unforeseen side effect.

332. It was the phone call you didn't want to make.

333. It was the phone call you never wanted to receive.

334. Why we agreed to a suicide pact.

335. "That's when I found myself deep in the forest, surrounded by grizzly bears."

336. Meeting at an advertising agency: the execs are trying to think of ways to sell something that's harmful.

337. A well known and established good fictional character turns evil. What is their motivation and in what ways are they evil?

338. "My life was going fine, and then she walked in the room."

339. A group of aliens crash land... on prehistoric Earth.

340. "I didn't believe her story, and then she brought me there."

341. The oddest funeral ever held.

342. They've made it clear you are no longer welcome at your favorite restaurant.

343. You're a bounty hunter in the old west, hot on the trail of the person you've been tracking for five years.

344. You discover a new button on the TV remote that wasn't there before.

345. Just by leaning against a random spot in your bedroom, you discover that there's a secret enclosure in the wall.

346. His reasons for being late were becoming increasingly unbelievable. When I finally demanded proof, he showed me a video on his phone.

347. After a blow to the head, you've realized you can now read minds.

348. A method actor who feels they must get into the roles they play is

cast as a serial killer.

349. Meeting at an advertising agency: The executives take on a controversial client who the world hates. They must make the world love them.

350. This prompt requires use of the internet. Go to Google Maps. Search for a country or location you've never been to that has Google Street View. Use Street View to "walk" around the streets and see what it looks like there. Imagine you are a person walking those streets. Write about your life there.

351. You and a group of friends survived the apocalypse. There is nothing that seems safe to eat. In your backpack you've been hiding a few oatmeal bars from them.

352. The moment you were humbled.

353. Your fortune cookie turned out to be right.

354. While driving home, you blink and realize night has turned to day... and that you are over 1,000 miles away from where you once were.

355. The government forces every civilian to get at least one bionic body part (internal or external) so that humans share something in common with androids.

356. As a royal taster, you must try all the Kings food before he does. You suspect the meal that was just delivered to him will likely kill you if you take a bite. If you announce this, you feel they will kill you thinking you poisoned the meal. How do you get out of this predicament? Do you?

357. You're a safe cracker; you thought you had seen all the treasures and odd objects in the world. Then you open one special vault.

358. "That was the fifth attempt on my life and that's just this morning!"

359. The cat is now able to control you.

360. "All we have to do is get to the roof."

361. After a near death experience, anyone you touch dies.

362. You are a muse, trying to determine who you should inspire next.

363. You are the same muse from prompt #362, trying to break off an attachment with a desperate artist.

364. Your first time at an alien strip club.

365. A solar blast rocked the Earth. Everything seemed normal right after. The next day, all the animals on the planet have gone forward about 10 evolutionary steps.

366. Two characters have made the difficult decision to elope.

367. You are trying to find the source of the clawing sound that has been plaguing you for weeks.

368. While on vacation, thousands of miles away from home, you find a prized childhood possession in a second hand shop. You know it's yours because your name is on the bottom.

369. The world as seen through a dog's eyes.

370. The world as seen through a cat's eyes.

371. "It reminded me of my home planet."

372. You decide to respond to an online posting that says: "Built a portal. Unsure where it leads. All electronic equipment fails when near. Need human subject."

373. You've found yourself stuck in the storyline of your favorite book.

374. "If you kill it, it will just come back angrier."

375. You've received a two minute heads up phone call from a friend. They simply stated: "Destroy all the evidence! Now! Hurry! Shred it all!"

376. You can't keep your opinions to yourself. You have to tell everyone what you think no matter what. What's life like?

377. The elevator has been stuck for hours; you're in there with three people. The conversation is getting tense.

378. They say revenge is a dish best served cold. You've waited ten years for this moment.

379. Waking up in the morgue.

380. It takes four keys to open the treasure. You have three of the keys, who has the fourth and how do you get it? What is the treasure?

381. Every day you lock your prized bicycle to the rack at the train station and go to work. One day you return from work and all you see is a broken lock, no bike. You decide to stake out the train station bicycle racks.

382. Upon waking, your spouse is missing. All traces of them are gone, including everyone's memory of them.

383. You come across something you wrote when you were 8 years old. It turns out to have been prophetic.

384. The last person you were ever closely related to is on their deathbed, while you are immortal.

385. You are a doctor who lets patients, who might be saved with a bit of extra effort; die on the operating table so you can harvest their organs.

386. "It was only then that I realized I was fighting for the wrong team."

387. You come home and see a family of people you've never met before inside. All the furniture... everything is different, you can tell through the window.

388. An insane leader triggers a nuclear holocaust. You somehow survive.

389. All the bad thoughts and evil inside you manifest into a copy of you. You have an interaction with them.

390. "That was how I overcame my phobia."

391. It's the future and "mood shirts" are a requirement for all citizens. Each color means a different emotion. What is life like now?

392. A locked file cabinet falls over, revealing...

393. One day you grow an inch and you are well into adulthood. The next day another inch. Keep this growing going as long as you like for the story.

394. You put poison in a drink, but someone you didn't intend it for begins to consume it.

395. The ground beneath you has started to give way. You run. Write the

pulse pounding narrative from start to finish as you try to outrun a giant sinkhole.

396. It's the first day at the new job and you discover...

397. A diver discovers a case of elixirs deep in the ocean that must be thousands of years old. The diver decides to drink one of the little vials.

398. You are sworn in as the President of the United States of America. Shortly thereafter, they bring you into an office where you get to know secrets no citizen gets to know.

399. "Oh, him? He designed Earth. You should meet Bob; his planet was way cooler."

400. A business opens that allows you to send a single text message to yourself in the past for 40% of what you earn in a year. What message do you send? What effect does it have?

Section 8: Writing Prompts #401-500

401. A priest hears the confessions of a serial killer. He ponders the dilemma of turning him in when God speaks to him and tells him not to.

402. Talk about your unlikely rise in professional football, from the concession stand to the big time on the field.

403. As a monarch, you are often required to settle disputes. The one before you today is tricky.

404. You're a radio DJ about to pull your final shift.

405. While digging to put down a foundation for a building, you discover something.

406. You go to the crossroads to make a deal with the devil.

407. After a life living in seclusion, hidden away by what you assumed was a cult, on your 18th birthday you discover what they've been preparing you for. You have been cloned from DNA that belonged to Jesus Christ.

408. You've discovered an oasis in the forest behind your house. Going here fully heals all your ailments. You want to tell people but know that telling them will likely tarnish the place.

409. You get a letter in the mail that says: If you read this entire letter, you will die. If you don't read the letter, someone you love will die.

410. "This was the first time I had ever seen my father shed a tear."

411. The story you shouldn't have overheard on the bus.

412. Write about someone that has done evil and unspeakable things, and then write from their perspective giving it a rational explanation where it is no longer evil.

413. Upon waking in the back of a police car, with your hands covered in blood and no memory of the past day, you begin to ask questions.

414. Teleportation has just been invented. You've signed up to be the first human trial.

415. A famous person is holding you captive and won't release you until they get what they want.

416. You discover that your lover is a top level assassin for the government and not a desk clerk, as you had originally thought.

417. Your brother tells you a secret and makes you promise to not reveal it. It proves to be a hard promise to keep.

418. "I was chosen to be the sacrifice. I made peace with my God."

419. Werewolves are real and dangerous; there are also millions of them. Write from the perspective of a regular person who must endure another night of the full moon.

420. A new and potent drug that has no side effects is released to the public, with no restrictions.

421. "They'll never find me here."

422. Every single day at exactly 2:30AM, the lights in your neighbor's living room flicker rapidly for a full minute.

423. Being a street musician wasn't all you thought it'd be. Describe a full day.

424. It wasn't snow falling outside, it was pure sugar.

425. Diving deep under water, you discover a new species.

426. You're reviewing footage of your security camera when you notice something that sends chills down your spine.

427. You look in your passport and see that it is stamped with places you have never been.

428. "It was no small feat escaping your clutches."

429. A letter from a man who thinks they're about to win a war. Then the next letter, weeks later, explaining that they have not.

430. There was only one way out, but your character had to make the ultimate sacrifice.

431. "The clown was drunk."

432. Write a poem that describes an epic journey a person once took long ago.

433. A strange portal has appeared in a mall and people gather around it.

434. People say that things like light bulbs could last forever without needing to be replaced, but that companies make it so they go out after a certain period. It is a practice called "Planned obsolescence." Write about the people who put such things in place.

435. A Native American in the early 1500's is hunting pilgrims. Write about his life.

436. The meeting I always keep, every Tuesday at 3PM, rain or shine.

437. The baby is not yours.

438. The stranger in the club leaned over and whispered in her ear...

439. You were climbing a cliff when your gear breaks and you're now hanging off the side using only your hands to try to save yourself.

440. There's blood on the underside of the set of cups you bought. How'd it get there?

441. As the leader of a crime syndicate, you get many requests from your underlings. Today is just another day of hearing requests from each leader.

442. You see a person who took your breath away the first time you met them but for the life of you, you can't remember their name. You must figure out a creative way to get that information from them.

443. "If I ever find the person who did this, they will rue the day I found them."

444. "My father's advice finally made sense."

445. A calm trip down a long river you've never been on before.

446. The last spaceship is leaving Earth. A necessary mass exodus. Outside of clothing and pets, you are allowed to bring any three items with you.

447. A cross country race against your arch nemesis in an effort to win one million dollars.

448. At a narcotics anonymous meeting, you see your first crush from high school. They don't seem to recognize you and you listen to their story.

449. "I don't know you. I don't want to know you. And I want to forget you exist!"

450. You make a New Years Resolution that sounds impossible to everyone but you are able to do it within the year.

451. There are common signs of bad luck: Breaking a mirror, walking under a ladder, opening an umbrella indoors. Create a new sign of bad luck and what happens to anyone who performs the action.

452. A breaking news story causes the anchor to weep uncontrollably.

453. An epic story about a man's choice between items on a menu. Make it sound like an odyssey.

454. A son or daughter you thought long dead is returned to you safely after ten years of having been gone.

455. Someone enters your car that you don't know.

456. "People will stop at nothing to get this. They won't be able to resist it or quit it."

457. The note left on the windshield of your car made you think.

458. A cell phone in your cabin begins ringing. You don't own a cell phone.

459. You've been in your bomb shelter for three months, supplies are running low and you've decided to go top side.

460. The shortcut home that wound up being an epic journey, one that nobody would ever believe.

461. "I'm going to give you until the count of twenty. Don't worry, I'll count real slow."

462. It has been twenty years since candy existed. You find a candy bar that has been preserved, it is worth untold fortunes, but you decide to eat it.

463. You're in witness relocation when at your job for a grocery store in this faraway place, someone recognizes you.

464. Two strangers bump into each other on the street. A purse falls on the ground and the woman who doesn't own the purse notices a picture of her husband has fallen out of the stranger's purse.

465. As a rapper, you have a reputation to uphold. However, what you portray is far from what you actually are as a person.

466. "The fog rolled in, this was our first warning sign."

467. A blizzard has forced you and your enemy into staying in the same house for three days straight. Ultimately, you become close friends.

468. The freak accident that shaped your main character.

469. Moving into a new home can be harrowing, but finding out it was the scene of a grisly murder adds a new wrinkle.

470. You're a serial arsonist. Explain your motivations and what you're doing on this particular night.

471. A robot feels its first emotion.

472. You've just awoken from cryogenic sleep. What year are you in? What's different? How do people react to you?

473. It's becoming apparent the medicine you took wasn't meant for you.

474. A vegan explains her choices to a hardcore meat eater.

475. You're asked by the love of your life to define what love means to you.

476. You've just been handed down a recipe book that's been in your family for generations. Reading the recipes, you discover something.

477. It's your tenth day on your trek to the North Pole. Why are you going there?

478. A pill is invented that could make people healthy and immortal. You're the head of a drug company who devotes their life to eliminate all evidence such a drug exists.

479. Your clone has just informed you they will be taking care of your life today.

480. It was a love triangle: A human, an alien and a mythical creature.

481. You're a knight in the middle of a quest. You come to a large door guarded by a dragon. The dragon states that you must answer three questions to continue.

482. A scientist created a new animal today.

483. An escalating war between two neighbors.

484. "She must like the taste of poison."

485. Your job was to flip on the mind control switch.

486. It was the ultimate proposal.

487. How I saw the world for only 100 dollars.

488. "You could smell the machine on her breath."

489. You're a scientist who has invented a box that when opened a different object from an alternate universe appears, you must put in a product from our universe for it to work.

490. The reason you still sleep with the lights on, even though you're middle-aged.

491. You find a thumb drive that contains code that would give you control over any site on the internet.

492. It was a crime of passion; you didn't mean to kill them!

493. You get a package in the mail from your father. Your father has been dead for ten years.

494. The sky was red today.

495. How I got rid of my stalker.

496. "It was the first time any of us saw the outside world."

497. Before any astronaut visits the moon, they must sign a document that contains startling details.

498. At last! Atlantis is discovered.

499. It is apparent someone has been living in your attic.

500. The final entry of a diary.

Section 8: Writing Prompts #501-600

501. A society without money. What is life like? How do you get goods?

502. You feel a presence behind you, as you slowly turn around you see...

503. "People may think I'm a joke, but this proves that they are all the laughing stock!"

504. The real reason the Titanic sank.

505. Aliens have imprisoned you in a zoo with one other human of the opposite sex.

506. You are granted three wishes. However, no matter how carefully worded you make them - each wish winds up with a severe downside.

507. You find yourself stranded in the middle of the ocean. How did you get there? What do you do next?

508. You've been told to keep an item secret for years. Then one day someone comes looking for it.

509. "If she's so smart, why does she have a fish on her head?"

510. Plastic surgeon figures out a brilliant idea to get new customers, but it backfires.

511. Narrate an illegal journey into a foreign country.

512. You are hired to go to extreme lengths to get a video scrubbed from the entirety of the internet.

513. A good deed winds up carrying the worst punishment.

514. A time traveler (from your era) is in the 1800's. They confide in someone that they are from the future. They attempt to explain modern times.

515. You're a security guard for a high rise building. The lights go out in the top three floors and you must investigate it.

516. It is the future; humans have all the free time they could possibly need since machines do every job.

517. A thrilling story unfolds via texting.

518. You are an "alien" and your planet isn't technologically advanced. Talk about the day the Earthlings landed.

519. "I know I am insane, but I am beyond my own control."

520. A hypnotist convinces an entire audience to perform a task.

521. You're attempting a strange world record. Talk about your training leading up to the event and the event itself.

522. A vertigo sufferer must save a woman dangling on the side of a building.

523. A cab driver hears an interesting phone conversation.

524. "I wish I never saw my therapist in that situation."

525. You are in the cockpit of a plane that is about to crash.

526. An inspired speech that is meant to rally the troops.

527. All technology is illegal.

528. Working off prompt #527, you are an underground dealer in technology. If you chose that to focus on with the previous prompt - then you are a purchaser of said illegal goods.

529. You're the antagonist and you finally have the protagonist at your mercy.

530. Write about your first day in jail.

531. Write about your last day in jail.

532. You are thrust back in time against your will 1,000 years in the past. The only things you traveled with: A gun, unlimited ammunition, vaccines.

533. On an epic quest, you face off against the final creature standing between you and glory.

534. You run a bar during the days of prohibition.

535. We've colonized Mars; you are welcoming the latest arrival of people from Earth. You are their tour guide.

536. You've never seen snow before in your fifty years of life, until today.

537. There's a mystery illness going around and you just got it. It turns your skin red with blue stripes.

538. You are holding someone for ransom; you send a carefully worded note.

539. The door to your closet opened, revealing a dark secret.

540. An anarchist decides to start a rebellion.

541. Cars are able to drive themselves in the future; your car decides to bring you to a destination you did not request.

542. While being tortured, you refuse to give any information your captors are seeking. Talk about the internal struggle you are facing.

543. You're a cheetah stalking your prey in large blades of grass. Talk about your ritual while hunting.

544. You get a text on your phone telling you to go to a random location you've never been to before... or else. Once there, you see an abandoned cell phone that starts ringing.

545. You're a legend in the town you're from, having earned a nickname. What is your nickname, how did you get it, how do people treat your triumphant return?

546. The man who designed our universe is about to accept the award for best design at a banquet in his honor.

547. An elf decides he is going to sabotage Christmas, he decides to wrap the worst things he can think of.

548. After an accident in the laboratory, you begin to mutate. These mutations are not desirable.

549. Death has decided to bring people back to life for an entire day. So, while nobody dies that day... people who suffered gruesome deaths are

then able to live again.

550. You are a problem solver, people call upon you at all hours of the day to help them out. The problem this time might be too hard for you to handle.

551. You are a scientist who studies the universe. You decide to build your own tiny universe in a box. After a weeks time, you discover that one of the tiny planets in the box not only has inhabitants, but they are far more advanced than us.

552. You are homeless, but you've come up with various ways to get free food. You're explaining how you go through a day to another recently homeless person.

553. You are told the reason you've had so much bad luck in your life is because of a bracelet you've worn for a long time. You attempt to destroy it, throw it away or otherwise be rid of it... but it's proving impossible.

554. The weather was treacherous, but he had no choice but to go out.

555. "It was only at this moment that I realized this wasn't a dream."

556. You enter the evil house at the end of the street on a dare.

557. They met each other by accident. It was a love that would be told through the ages.

558. You had held onto and protected the object for twenty years.

559. You've heard of bad breakups, but this one left three people dead, ten injured and three cities completely devastated.

560. His obituary seemed to pose more questions than give answers. It explains why so many people keep trying to dig up the grave.

561. Your first time stealing something isn't going exactly as you had planned.

562. You've been hypnotized. A particular word turns you into something you can't control.

563. You work for a government agency that monitors everyone. You use the resources to spy on people in your life during your lunch break.

564. "It was my earliest memory, but I have no idea why I'd remember such a trivial thing."

565. You have no idea why, but you have a compulsion to swallow small shiny objects. You can't seem to control it.

566. The date was going so well, but what you saw in the bedroom shook you to the core.

567. An architect who has cause to question precisely what he's been asked to design.

568. You've sold all your possessions and decide to trek across the country in your van.

569. It is your first day as a superhero and you agonize over what your super name should be.

570. While doing a random home inspection of a hoarder, a pile of random items falls on you. It is now day three of your attempt to get out of this mess of a place.

571. Telekinesis is a fact of future life. Everyone is able to do it. What is life like in this new society?

572. You are the dictator of a small country. You've decided to do something that is evil to your people.

573. The assistant to a famed evil doer decides to think up his own evil schemes, to comical results.

574. A minor character from a famous story decides to go on his own epic adventure.

575. The world stops rotating one day, leaving one side in perpetual light, the other side in perpetual darkness.

576. An astronomer notices that the stars of the universe are going out at a rapid rate.

577. You're about to storm a castle with other ninjas, in an attempt to overthrow the kingdom.

578. While in a laundromat, you wind up grabbing someone else's clothes. When you get home you realize the clothes just look better than what you

had before, so you decide to selfishly keep the ill gotten threads. What you don't realize is that you look strikingly similar to the person who the outfits previously belonged to. This is not a good thing.

579. You refuse ten million dollars.

580. "Even though he's dead, I wish I could throw a banana at him one more time."

581. The house you've rented turns out to be a notorious crack den.

582. The most unusual profession you can think of. Write about your workday.

583. Your character has passed on, their loved ones are cleaning out their possessions and come across a few startling belongings.

584. When the wedding ceremony got to the question of objection to the marriage, someone raised their hand.

585. Your attempt to stop a stranger from killing themselves by jumping off a bridge.

586. You're the first person to get a brain implant that allows you to make calls, take pictures, everything that you can do with a phone with your mind.

587. You abduct children and sell them to couples desperately seeking to adopt a child. Justify your actions and go through a typical day.

588. "I saw Death, but he couldn't see me."

589. She was the most beautiful person in the world, but she made certain there were no mirrors in her house.

590. You carry your childhood blanket with you wherever you go, not for comfort but because it is magical.

591. The first person to create fire, how they did it and their reaction.

592. If you could turn back time, you would not have invented that thing you invented.

593. You are a reporter who must have touched upon something because you've just received your first death threat.

594. You were adopted and are finally successful. Your birth parents decide to contact you at this point.

595. You're a prisoner of war and it is your fifth year in a small cage.

596. "It was like no time had passed at all. I was as angry as I was when we last met."

597. No hospital will treat you for what you have.

598. Your nightmares start invading reality, a little bit at a time.

599. The one thing you swore you would never do, you are now being forced to do.

600. You are chosen to be the sacrificial offering for an evil creature. Talk about preparing yourself for this event.

Section 9: Writing Prompts #601-700

601. When trying to get through security at an airport, you are mistaken for a terrorist.

602. While opening gifts at a birthday party, you start to open a box everyone swears they did not place there.

603. It's always strange to see a boss, teacher or other person of authority in your life during the course of your regular day or weekend. However, where you saw them this time was extremely awkward.

604. For once, procrastination saved your life.

605. "The first thing they teach you in Time Travel Academy is to be careful where you step."

606. You are a woman who has just been stood up on a potential date. It turns out to be the best night ever, though.

607. You are a man who was about to go out on a date with the woman in prompt #606. A series of extreme circumstances get in the way.

608. You are a motivational speaker, but during a seminar trying to motivate people, one person finally demoralizes you.

609. The lengths you go to in an attempt to stop yourself from the vicious cycle of overeating have grown increasingly elaborate.

610. You are a star in the heavens that is about to go supernova.

611. "The child would have to save the Earth."

612. You're finally successful and you decide to rub it in the face of someone who doubted you.

613. You are known as "The Chameleon." You are able to change your appearance. What services do you provide?

614. You come out as a "furry" to your family.

615. After having one too many to drink, you come up with a plan to quit

your job in an epic fashion.

616. It turns out that Heaven is real: You are trying to justify all the bad things in life to get access.

617. You're the owner of a candy shop; a new candy comes in that people can't get enough of.

618. "You've got two minutes to make a decision."

619. You don't know why you stopped being friends, one day you find out precisely why they hate you.

620. You cause a huge car crash. What were the events leading up to the crash? What was the result?

621. The sound of rain fills your ears.

622. The kidnapper's voice sounded familiar.

623. You notice your front door lock has been broken.

624. You are given the option to relive a single day of your choosing from the past, with the promise to return to present day - with your timeline forever changed.

625. You notice the same person has been following you all day.

626. The voices in your head are now in control of your body.

627. You invent a machine that allows people to track who got them sick.

628. The sleaziest person on Earth.

629. The pregnancy test in the bathroom proves what you thought.

630. The thing that haunted you when you were a kid is back again, years later.

631. "He had never experienced snow before."

632. Everyone takes pity on you. If only you knew why.

633. You're the person whose house kids run past for fear that you might see them.

634. You work at the coat check of a fine restaurant. Something falls out of the pocket of one of the coats you've collected that makes you call the police.

635. The real reason people have freckles.

636. "What was interesting wasn't what was there, it was what wasn't there."

637. "It sounds awful, but I would do it again if given the chance."

638. You're in line at an unemployment office when someone comes up to you with an odd job proposal.

639. The unspoken relationship between you and the girl on the bus.

640. You are a parasite, gleefully entering a new host.

641. There are two shadows when there should only be one.

642. Your character has to rely on their back-up plan.

643. The acid rain started pouring without warning.

644. The worst part about the injury you recently received.

645. "We've been waiting for you to make it here. This will be relatively painless."

646. A video you made has gone viral.

647. You've been sucked out of a plane and are falling towards Earth.

648. Two people walk into a bar, only one leaves alive.

649. You find your friend naked, writing on the floor and covered in a layer of snow. It's the middle of summer.

650. You are a heavy sleeper. You keep devising new ways to get yourself up in the morning.

651. "We thought you'd be asleep."

652. Modern technology is all based off technology brought back to 1970

by a time traveler. You are that time traveler.

653. You have distilled fear into an ingestible liquid.

654. Something the public should never have been made aware of is leaked online.

655. There were only two people left on the train. You... and the person that has been staring at you the entire ride.

656. You're a soldier in a combat zone who gets his first kill. You are worried because you enjoyed killing the person.

657. "You're an Earthling? I'm so sorry about your planet."

658. Something is eating you alive.

659. You are an amnesiac that nobody is able to identify.

660. "I was the last one to know."

661. The fable of the man trapped in the walls around the city.

662. Something finally gets the nihilistic person to feel something.

663. Write from the point of view of a bird that must fight other, larger birds over any food that comes their way.

664. When you went for your job interview, the entire building was empty. Then you went next door and that building was empty. Come to think of it, the entire city was deserted.

665. You learn there are different levels to Hell. You are shown every level, and then brought to your own.

666. Satan has decided to do something good for the people living on Earth.

667. You're in a secret branch of the government; you've been given an assignment to terminate a citizen. It turns out to be an old teacher who turned your life around.

668. You were left for dead on the roadside, you recovered in the hospital and your memory came back. Write about your revenge.

669. The quest your character goes through to find their birth parents does not end as they expected.

670. The reason why the well dressed man had his hat in hand and was asking strangers for money.

671. The ultimate torture device.

672. The day you had been dreading winds up being the best day of your life.

673. The rapture happens; people are lifted up to the heavens. However, lots of people are left on Earth. There is no apocalypse following the rapture. What happens to the world and everyone on it?

674. You've got just one fragment to an ancient machine that could change the world.

675. "They say if at first you don't succeed, try try try again. I had a different take."

676. While driving along a lonely road, you glance at the time. When you glance again a moment later, you notice two hours have passed.

677. "This room was locked, every window barred, every entrance covered. How did you get in here?"

678. They say that machines could one day turn against us. Talk about a revolution of the machines, but only machines that aren't humanoid in any sense. Toasters, microwaves, you name it. They all turn on us.

679. The old person went back to their place of youth and everything had changed, except one thing in particular.

680. The place hadn't been lived in for years; there is a thick layer of dust throughout the entire house. The living room is completely empty and has as much dust as every other room in the house, except for a single pair of footprints in the center of the room.

681. "It was then that I discovered: I could not die."

682. A beautiful death.

683. You've cleaned a lot of hotel rooms in your life, but nothing could prepare you for what you walked in on today.

684. You exit your house one day and notice that everyone is frozen in place.

685. The last thing you saw before you went blind.

686. The last thing you heard before you went deaf.

687. You are the person who invents the thing we all take for granted today.

688. The gas ran out, the nearest town is 100 miles away, this is the last place you wanted to be stranded.

689. The smell of sulfur is what woke you up.

690. "I've captured all of them."

691. Alternate universe: ghosts are an accepted part of life.

692. The final ingredient needed to cast the spell.

693. The door did not lead to my bedroom anymore.

694. A graffiti artist finds himself doing much riskier pieces.

695. "She had been rich her entire life, but when she turned 30, she gave away every last penny."

696. In a densely populated city, you yearn to be noticed.

697. He keeps his heart in a box at the top of the bookcase.

698. The second ice age.

699. The way you got that scar.

700. A jealous lover goes down your list of contacts, calling everyone that they think you might be seeing. One number they call just has three long tones and silence. They think nothing of it, but one minute later a person calls back and says they will be at your location in five minutes.

Section 10: Writing Prompts #701-800

701. No matter how the reader cut the deck, the tarot cards kept saying the same thing.

702. She followed the buzzing sound.

703. A poem about loss.

704. Ever since the donated organ was placed in your body, you've been experiencing the oddest side effect.

705. The mist billows out your mouth as you submerge your body into the freezing water.

706. You take up a challenge to be dropped in a country you don't know, where people speak a language you don't speak, and the only thing in your possession is 10 dollars of whatever currency you decide. You need to figure out how to get home.

707. Here's another money prompt: You're given $5 and told you have 2 hours to increase the amount of money you have as part of a contest.

708. You've no choice; you have to enlist the help of a criminal to get what you need.

709. Going through a body x-ray machine, they stop you. It seems there's something implanted in your stomach.

710. The story of reincarnated lovers.

711. A teenager writes a heartfelt love letter to the girl he has a crush on. He slips the note in the wrong girl's locker.

712. The person who revels in other peoples misery.

713. All the patients of an insane asylum escape.

714. Take a character from an older fiction and place them in modern times.

715. How a game of solitaire turned deadly.

716. You find yourself in a sensory depravation chamber.

717. Alternate universe: There is nowhere in the world that isn't covered by a camera of some sort. You must figure out how to pull off a heist successfully.

718. You are able to trick a child into thinking that you can read their mind.

719. You are a store owner, but your store is a front for something else.

720. Framing someone else for a crime.

721. The miracle cure will save you from death, but you will become homicidal.

722. The slave that became the slave owner of his former "master".

723. The ruins of modern civilization are uncovered by a future society.

724. The meaning behind crop circles.

725. Creaking footsteps down the stairs in your house. You live alone.

726. Entering the camouflaged city.

727. You discover an old leather bound journal belonging to someone you've never met.

728. "I have no soul, this isn't an opinion... this is fact."

729. A person gets an awesome power, but each day has to eat an increasingly more substantial amount of food.

730. You weren't sure where the footprints would lead, but you followed them anyway.

731. A quiet argument.

732. You thought you could keep your promise, but this was an extreme condition.

733. Another "Midas touch" type of prompt: Everyone you touch becomes hopelessly in lust with you, the only way to stop their obsession

with you is...

734. The river of blood.

735. "The crack of the whip ruined the mood."

736. Everyone who has ever lived is suddenly alive again, at their prime age and health. (For statistical purposes, at the time of this writing the number would be 108 billion.)

737. A child who has been mute his entire life finally speaks.

738. You live on a flat planet. You are at a tourist spot overlooking the edge.

739. Two kids find a dead body on abandoned train tracks.

740. The abandoned school would be the perfect location.

741. You're driving about 150MPH (241Kmh) on the highway.

742. Your family has long since turned their back on you. One day you become filthy rich and well known.

743. "For each minute that passes, you lose another limb. Your choice."

744. You discover your tombstone.

745. The man who lost the ability to sleep.

746. You're an animal who has witnessed a human killing another human. You understand how wrong it is and you want desperately to communicate to someone about it and who did it.

747. The last tree on the planet.

748. You're in a plane crash. Six of you survive. It is now day seven and you start to realize the group of survivors is discussing the options of killing and eating you.

749. "When I looked at the palms of my hand, a red X has been scrawled on each."

750. In the future, when you are conscripted in the army, you are in for life. Your character has been in for forty years and doesn't know where

the man ends and the machine begins, having had so many parts replaced.

751. Write the most riveting story from your autobiography.

752. You're the last person on Earth... but somehow the internet still seems to work.

753. A librarian that is able to teleport into the world of any book at will.

754. Your father wishes someone else were their son.

755. As a Viking, you've seen your fair share of war and carnage. Your heart is not in the next battle.

756. The blog of a person desperately seeking communication with the outside world.

757. Putting the old gang together for one last hurrah.

758. Two prisoners bond over a similar passion.

759. A common setting is one man in a jury trying to convince everyone of the innocence of a defendant. Try the reverse, someone trying to convince everyone of the guilt of someone.

760. A hacker trying to infiltrate the government's servers finally gets in. They immediately wish they had not.

761. It turns out that the painting you are looking at is a portal.

762. You have the sinking suspicion that you're being stalked.

763. You're a stalker, stalking your next obsession.

764. "An 80's song came on that really encapsulated what had happened."

765. You've killed your son in the heat of the moment.

766. You find out that you are a character in a game.

767. The new kid at school was weird, to say the least.

768. A misdirected e-mail to a stranger leads to a romance.

769. You discover a way to communicate with those that have passed on. Anyone that you want to contact appears on the other side of this supernatural glass you've made. You create a business out of it.

770. Alternate universe: Something we consider normal in this universe is considered taboo in the alternate universe.

771. A person who wants to get into a fight finally gets their wish.

772. You've become a recluse because of your newfound ability: Every object you pick up that isn't yours gives you an unfortunately deep insight into the life of the last person who touched it.

773. You get a letter in the mail. The letter is the first clue to a scavenger hunt of some kind.

774. The priceless artifact that shattered on the ground.

775. A group of kids are terrorizing the neighborhood with harmless pranks.

776. You are a kleptomaniac who steals the weirdest things.

777. "I shouldn't have consumed that water from Saturn."

778. A comical situation turns horrific.

779. A horrific situation turns comical.

780. Your life, flashing before your eyes.

781. You are a carrier pigeon, carrying an important message during WWII.

782. You are an astronaut on the first mission outside of our galaxy. Once you leave the galaxy, you notice a sphere off in the distance. The sphere, as you get closer, turns out to be a bio-dome of some sorts.

783. You rescue someone from certain death. They are recuperating in your bed and begin muttering something in their feverish state.

784. The government creates a drug that is meant to control the populace.

785. Every day for years you've had the same dream, it ends at the same

point. One day you get to live that dream and this is the time where knowing the end of the dream would have helped you.

786. The fate of the universe rests on your ability to answer three simple questions.

787. The tale of the cursed wedding ring.

788. You are able to put your consciousness into anyone else's body when you are asleep.

789. You create a gun that has the ability to freeze people in time.

790. Though you planned it carefully, your victim somehow lived.

791. People say their hair has a life of its own. Yours actually does.

792. You are a new recruit for a secret base hidden by the government.

793. Being independently wealthy, you've decided to create a utopia on an island, devoid of most modern technology.

794. You are celebrity photographer. But the one video you capture that would be worth millions you question ever releasing.

795. We've all seen shows where someone flashes their badge and commandeers a car. The action always follows that police officer. Write about the person whose car just got legally stolen.

796. You are a doctor who has witnessed many births. This birth, however...

797. Underneath a famous landmark.

798. "I'm just pretending to be sick."

799. Every day, at precisely the same time, you feel a sharp pain in the same spot.

800. The mirror in your bathroom gives you a view to another universe every day. You've grown used to it to the point that it annoys you and have it covered with a towel. One day, a pizza delivery person asks to use your bathroom. Not remembering the mirror, you grant access to the bathroom. He removes the towel.

Section 11: Writing Prompts #801-900

801. Your choice between the lesser of two evils.

802. There's only one library in the future on Earth. It's a massive building with its own zip code.

803. A successful killer who is always unsuccessful at killing themselves.

804. The birth of the universe.

805. The FBI has dragged you in for questioning.

806. You go to extreme lengths to prove someone wrong.

807. Entertaining the King proved to be difficult.

808. The most important invention of the next one hundred years.

809. You are a person who was literally raised by wolves.

810. There is a hearse that has been driving through the neighborhood everyday. There is no funeral or graveyard within ten miles.

811. The last dragon's egg.

812. Alternate Universe: Computers have never existed.

813. You find yourself unexpectedly rescuing someone from the jaws of death.

814. Write from the perspective of a people trafficker.

815. The poem that won awards and sparked so many to love poetry again.

816. You are a train robber in the wild west.

817. The delivery person was five hours late.

818. Write from the perspective of someone who just did a hit and run.

819. The road signs you had been following all along were false. Someone led you here.

820. You know your client is guilty as sin.

821. A prison everyone desires to go to.

822. Your house appears to be moving.

823. The genie had granted many wishes over millennia. Write about the one person whose wishes they enjoyed granting the most.

824. The misunderstood monster.

825. Your reconditioning is coming to an end. Write about your brain washing.

826. Two powerful Gods get in the ultimate clash on Earth in modern times.

827. The black object under your bed.

828. Everyone falls unconscious in the entire world, except you.

829. A new law is causing an uproar.

830. Alternate universe: You are the person in charge of choosing what the weather is going to be like on any given day.

831. Nature speaks to you.

832. You find yourself stranded on the surface of Mars.

833. You're a hostage negotiator trying to negotiate your latest release.

834. There's something you do every day that's highly illegal. (Slight constraint on this one: You can't write about something like pirating things on the internet.)

835. The assassins apprentice.

836. You've unleashed an ancient monster - on purpose.

837. Write about the first person to ever decide to eat meat.

838. An alcoholic enters a bar he's never seen before. It's populated by the ghosts of people killed as a direct result of alcohol.

839. There's a well known thing called "The 27 Club" - famous people who seem to die at the age of 27. Jimi Hendrix, Janis Joplin, Jim Morrison, Kurt Cobain, Amy Winehouse and more. Write about a reality where they didn't die, but that the 27 Club serves a different purpose.

840. There is only one safe zone on Earth and you are rushing towards it.

841. You must break the heart of someone you love in order for them to live.

842. A vampire is trying to explain the gravity of the choice between dying mortal and being immortal.

843. You've developed a device that, when attached, turns a person who is homicidal into a functioning member of society.

844. While tuning the radio in your car, you come across a station that should not exist.

845. You're an animal activist who is set on sneaking into a testing facility to release animals.

846. A father confronts the daughter's choice of a suitor at gunpoint.

847. You're in a rock band, preparing for the most important gig of your life.

848. Reincarnation is a reality; you're on your tenth reincarnation and remember all your previous lives. You realize that in each body, you've been murdered.

849. It's 1690 and you're a pirate. You gain access and control of a silver ship. Inside the ship are items of modern times.

850. When going through your photographs, you notice a strange person in five separate images. These pictures were each years apart.

851. The knowledgeable tour guide to a cavernous underground bunker.

852. You find yourself in a maze, desperate to escape.

853. You've been put in charge of planning the most elaborate funeral.

854. You are in a business meeting and must convince everyone that your idea isn't insane.

855. Taking the world's most dangerous person into custody.

856. The suitcase you've been ordered to deliver appears to be making a ticking sound.

857. Everyone in your life is an actor employed by the government.

858. Working nights has exposed you to a different view of the world.

859. You are a person capable of traveling through different universes with ease. In one universe, a celebrity who died young is very much alive.

860. While going through a bookstore, an item catches your eye. You immediately feel the urge to buy it. When flipping through the pages, you discover a note scrawled on the side.

861. "That's the reason I don't go outside anymore."

862. The nanny has some specific demands.

863. The warrior returns home from battle only to realize that life is different.

864. Crossing off names on a list.

865. The music you create has the ability to bend people to your will.

866. In the dusty attic, you discover an old album of pictures. It seems to be a catalog of your life. Then you notice current pictures you don't recall. Then pictures of things yet to come.

867. While cleaning the litter box for a cat, you discover something that isn't from your pet.

868. You are a scam artist, you've stolen cars by pretending you're a valet, and you've taken people for hundreds of dollars by putting a skimmer on ATM card scanners. This new scheme of yours is brilliant.

869. The identities of every online troll are released by the government.

870. The most awkward time to find out that you're immortal.

871. Your main character has their worst fear validated.

872. A swirling portal appears while you are on the toilet.

873. A story that is conveyed almost entirely by dialogue.

874. While doing a hallucinogen, your character has the most profound vision quest.

875. The world's first floating city was not a complete success.

876. Demons discuss how to make life on Earth a little bit worse.

877. The main character somehow speaks every single language.

878. "If you give it water, it will kill us."

879. Two women bond over the evil man they both loved.

880. You've organized a militia. Today is the day you've prepared to launch a rebellion.

881. A computer repair technician decides to peek at the files of the computer he's taking care of.

882. You are a newspaper columnist. You feel you have integrity. You are told to write a puff piece for the owner of the company, even though you've just discovered something negative about them.

883. The cruise ship you are on passes through the Bermuda Triangle.

884. A most harrowing adventure at sea.

885. Someone takes credit for all your hard work, for some reason you let them.

886. You are an artist, someone from the future has travelled back to tell you that your work is going to be worth millions in the future. How does this affect you?

887. You have a vision for how cities should look in the future, how do people react to this vision?

888. Staging a fake kidnapping to get money out of your rich parents.

889. A promiscuous person is weighing the options of making a living out of it.

890. You find the reason you've been getting so many headaches lately.

891. Alternate Universe: Dinosaurs coexist with humans.

892. You're about to get away with it, then comes the surprise witness.

893. You are trying not to laugh during a serious situation; it only gets more difficult as time passes.

894. There's a sound, it starts off small but it's getting closer.

895. You found the note when you got home, everything else was gone.

896. The potion you just drank was supposed to make you cooler.

897. Your phone talks to you.

898. Your radar shows something is closing in on your location.

899. "Everyone here has the same affliction, so be quiet and calm."

900. Someone's reanimating murder victims so they can get revenge.

Section 12: Writing Prompts #901-1000

901. You've developed an allergy to water.

902. There are three spontaneous combustions. The only common thread between each person who spontaneously combusted is you.

903. An alien's first trip to Earth is on Halloween. It knows nothing of the holiday.

904. Everyone thinks you are dead, you decide to let them keep thinking that.

905. The whole neighborhood knows what the corner store is actually a front for.

906. The novel you are reading sounds familiar. The more you read on, the more it becomes apparent that the character you're reading about is you. That's right, I'm talking to you. The person reading this prompt right now. This entire novel is about you.

907. You are the main attraction at an old timey carnival side show.

908. You sleep for a single hour a day, once a week, thanks to a special drug trial you are on. This begins to have a profound effect on your life.

909. A war breaks out for control over the colonization of a newly discovered inhabitable planet.

910. Alternate universe: Everyone on the planet speaks the same language.

911. You gain control over a magical door. All you have to do is write a location, any location, at the top of the door and when you open it, it brings you to where you've written.

912. The first time falling in love, years after the death of your soulmate.

913. You're a poor man trying to seduce rich women.

914. A doctor removes something strange from a patient.

915. The things you have tried to quit smoking are numerous, you finally hit on something that helps you quit.

916. You've been lured into a trap!

917. The house you've broken into has a cellar filled with imprisoned people.

918. You walk by a lever at work. It is there every day in the same position. One day your curiosity gets the better of you and you pull the lever.

919. "Don't raise your voice. It will wake the dead."

920. The final song ever written.

921. When a routine fire drill begins, you get the feeling it is anything but routine.

922. For some reason, everyone finds your obituary to be hilarious.

923. You become a pacifist, even though you are the target of a gang every day.

924. A purchased typewriter reveals a secret. A message written many years ago, typed on a small strip of paper, lodged inside.

925. Switching places as your twin was meant to be fun, but this was an awful outcome.

926. You remove an important and integral piece from something.

927. The thing that was finally worth selling your soul for.

928. A wealthy man suddenly becomes poor.

929. "I'm you from the future. You're going to have to let me handle the next ten minutes."

930. You discover why people gave you that nickname they gave you.

931. As if a switch went on, everyone who used to be evil is now good, and everyone who used to be good is now evil.

932. Another Earth appears in the sky, we are told our inhabitants were a

mistake and the replacement Earth will be taking the current Earths place.

933. You try to lose on purpose because the consolation prize looks better than the grand prize.

934. You and some friends play a deadly drunken game.

935. "I'm not sure how you got here, but I'll make sure you leave."

936. You have a strong feeling the train you are on will crash. You begin a frantic attempt at stopping it.

937. As you are walking down the street at night, the lights begin to go out one by one.

938. You've got a birthmark and it has some meaning.

939. You finally meet one of your idols that you've obsessed over.

940. You've discovered a hidden talent that seems useless to you.

941. You are the entity that controls time itself.

942. The city behind the waterfall.

943. Think of the most ridiculous title for a story you can, and then write a story for that title. A personal favorite of mine is the story by Harlan Ellison titled: "Repent, Harlequin!" Said the Ticktockman.

944. In limbo between life and death.

945. "The man inside the box told me to."

946. Every day you see the old woman leave a plate of food on her front porch.

947. You are the creature that gets summoned at a slumber party.

948. Why the car had seven notches on the side of the door.

949. The overwhelming beauty of what you are painting.

950. Alternate universe: Being a witch or a warlock is the norm here. Not being one is strange.

951. "You're going to die tonight."

952. You are someone who ignores all warnings and signs proclaiming danger.

953. Trying to get through to a child who everyone else has given up on.

954. Your character has decided if they can't be famous, they might as well be infamous.

955. A famous person is actually a spy for the government.

956. Write about the zombie apocalypse, from the viewpoint of a world leader.

957. You took the wrong medication.

958. There is a message written on the bathroom stall: "Please call this number" with a phone number underneath. You feel oddly compelled to do so.

959. It was a mistake to look up your family history.

960. Write about something people would consider amazing, but make it sound mundane.

961. Write about something mundane, but make it sound like the most exciting thing ever.

962. You are trying to resist the effects of a love potion.

963. "I've been sent from the future to give you this message."

964. The first machine to kill itself.

965. The search for the perfect tea leaf.

966. For some reason, you are listing every mistake you have ever made.

967. ALTERNATE UNIVERSE: Cell phones existing during the time of World War II.

968. Humans are no longer the top of the food chain.

969. You are at the gates of Heaven, but first you must pass an interview.

970. You've abducted people and have them hidden under the floorboards of your house. You get an unexpected house call.

971. Write a story that is about isolation.

972. You're a doctor who has been given full permission to do any medical experiments you want on prisoners deemed too evil to ever see the light of day again.

973. Satan has announced himself to the world and is about to give a press conference.

974. "Don't do it. He's not worth it!"

975. You are a health inspector, what you discover at one restaurant shakes you to the core.

976. Getting caught trespassing.

977. In the future, we are able to download e-mails and other communications in our mind. One day, the worst e-mail virus gets sent out.

978. You receive the order to eliminate yourself.

979. The first time a character takes a hallucinogenic drug.

980. You take a chance and pick up a hitchhiker.

981. You are known as a "pick up artist." Write about your exploits.

982. Think of the weirdest title for a story. Then write the story to fit the title.

983. Write about a character that is having the worst string of bad luck due to simple miscommunication. Make their day get progressively worse.

984. It's 2AM and you get a call from someone you've not spoken to in ten years.

985. Everyone thinks you are in a coma, but you can hear everything everyone says at your bedside.

986. We are given the ability to access every thought and memory we

have ever had. Talk about loading some of your earliest memories on to the computer and watching them.

987. Create a funny nickname for a character. Then write a biography about that character and how they got the peculiar nickname.

988. The lightning strike had a strange side effect on you.

989. In the future, aliens have long since taken over the Earth. According to a study by the aliens, human kind is on the brink of extinction.

990. "Oh to be young again... again."

991. You enter a room that is covered in blood. Not a spot is free of it.

992. "If we do this, we both have to commit to it. There's no turning back."

993. Every morning you wake at 5:34AM. You hear no sounds, nobody lives in your house, and you have no alarms set. Yet, like clockwork, you wake at this time.

994. You've decided to crash a party down the street. You didn't realize it was THAT kind of party.

995. You are poor and you're trying everything you can think of to meet and hook a rich mate.

996. You unwittingly violate a clause in a contract you never bothered to read, to dire consequence.

997. Write about two brothers who meet on the battlefield on opposite sides of the fight.

998. You awaken, trapped inside a casket.

999. A person who has been stalked for years by the same person decides to start stalking them.

1000. You've discovered that you have a natural ability to create the most beautiful art (be it painting, writing, music, etc.) that has ever been experienced. Upon going to the doctor, you discover that the reason for this newfound talent is a brain tumor. You must make a decision between your health and your art.

Section 13: Thanks

I hope this book has somehow helped you write something. I want to thank you, the writer, for reading and responding to these prompts. If you need help or guidance at any time, my personal email address is ryanandrewkinder@gmail.com. I may not be the quickest person in the world when responding, but I'll certainly try. I can't edit your book for you though, it was a tough enough time editing this book, even with the generous assistance of Sarah Kinder, who helped immensely. If you notice any mistakes, nobody is perfect and I blame Microsoft Word.

Another thanks to Christopher Short for the resdesign of the cover for this book. My previous cover wasn't all that great, but this one looks like an actual cover!

A final thought: I have a personal notebook that I've been writing prompts in for a long time, enough that I will have to put out future volumes! Be sure to look for that in the future. Until then, look for inspiration everywhere you go and you will find it. Also, keep being awesome.

Yours,

Ryan Andrew Kinder
ryanandrewkinder@gmail.com
@rykinder on twitter

Section 14: Copyright Stuff You Probably Don't Care About

CPSIA information can be obtained
at www.ICGtesting.com
Printed in the USA
BVHW03s1319211018
530586BV00005BA/5/P

9 781500 910662